Sesame Street® Self-Care

Be a Friend

Learn about Healthy Friendships with Sesame Street

Whitney Sanderson

Lerner Publications ◆ Minneapolis

In this series, young readers will learn different ways they can take care of themselves! Come along as Elmo and his *Sesame Street* friends explore how healthy habits—like eating well and expressing your feelings—help you grow smarter, stronger, and kinder.

Sincerely,
the Editors at Sesame Workshop

Table of Contents

What Is a Friend?

A friend is someone who you have fun with and who you care about. Learn how you can be a kind friend!

Snuffy is my best friend!

Fun with Friends

Playing and spending time with friends is important. You can invite a friend to have fun with you!

Elmo likes having playdates with Abby.
I like playing with you too, Elmo!

Friends can play games together. They can make up new games or even play pretend.

Let’s pretend this box is a race car!

Friends take turns and share. Sharing is a way to show that you care about each other.

Elmo and Julia are sharing blocks!

When a friend is having a big feeling, sometimes you can tell by looking at their face and body. Helping your friends is a kind thing to do.

When Bert feels sad, I give him a hug to help him feel better.

Friends might like different things than you do. You can play different things and still be friends.

When friends disagree, you can work together to find a solution. You can take turns saying what happened and how you feel.

I feel disappointed because we want to play different things. I want to paint.

And I want to play tag.

You can think of different ways to solve a problem. Sometimes the first idea doesn't work. You can come up with new ideas and do what everyone thinks is fair.

I have an idea. Let's paint first, then play tag.
I love that idea!

We can all be good friends! More friends mean more people to laugh and play with.

Healthy You!

Together with a friend, write or draw a list of things you like about each other. Then share your lists.

Glossary

disagree: to have different ideas or opinions

friend: someone who you have fun with and who you care about

share: to use something with others or take turns using it

solution: a way to solve a problem

Read More

Murray, Julie. *Friendship*. Minneapolis: Abdo Kids, 2020.

Peterson, Christy. *Many Ways to Be a Friend.* Minneapolis: Lerner Publications, 2023.

Sepulveda, Fabiola. *How to Be a Friend.* Huntington Beach, CA: Teacher Created Materials, 2024.

Photo Acknowledgments

Image credits: Anna Frank/Getty Images, p. 4; THEPALMER/Getty Images, p. 6; goir/Shutterstock, p. 8 (box); a-clip/Getty Images, p. 9; Dmytro Zinkevych/Alamy, p. 10; kali9/Getty Images, pp. 12, 17; FatCamera/Getty Images, pp. 15, 18; Kevin Dodge/Getty Images, p. 20.

Design element: Dedraw Studio/Shutterstock

Index

For Faisal

Lerner Publications Company
An imprint of Lerner Publishing Group, Inc.
241 First Avenue North
Minneapolis, MN 55401 USA

For reading levels and more information, look up this title at www.lernerbooks.com.

Main body text set in Mikado. Typeface provided by HVD.

Editor: Annie Zheng

Library of Congress Cataloging-in-Publication Data

Names: Sanderson, Whitney, author.
Title: Be a friend : learn about healthy friendships with Sesame Street / Whitney Sanderson.
Description: Minneapolis : Lerner Publications, [2025] | Series: Sesame Street self-care | Includes bibliographical references and index. | Audience: Ages 4–8 | Audience: Grades K–1 | Summary: "Playing and spending time with friends is fun, and learning how to be a good friend is important. From sharing and taking turns to solving problems together, young readers learn ways to be a friend"— Provided by publisher.
Identifiers: LCCN 2024009493 (print) | LCCN 2024009494 (ebook) | ISBN 9798765643730 (library binding) | ISBN 9798765662434 (paperback) | ISBN 9798765657911 (epub)
Subjects: LCSH: Friendship in children—Juvenile literature. | Friendship—Juvenile literature.
Classification: LCC BF723.F68 S256 2025 (print) | LCC BF723.F68 (ebook) | DDC 177/.62083—dc23/eng/20240603

LC record available at https://lccn.loc.gov/2024009493
LC ebook record available at https://lccn.loc.gov/2024009494

Manufactured in the United States of America
2-1012566-52414-4/10/2025